D1045022

Eeeeeek!

by Patty Wolcott
illustrated by Ned Delaney

JAMES PRENDERGAST LIBRARY ASSOCIATION
E READER C.2

Addison-Wesley

*"To all children
who are learning to read"*

FIRST READ-BY-MYSELF BOOKS
by PATTY WOLCOTT

Beware of a Very Hungry Fox
The Cake Story
Double-Decker, Double-Decker, Double-Decker Bus
The Dragon and the Wild Fandango
EEEEEEK!
The Forest Fire
I'm Going to New York to Visit the Queen
The Marvelous Mud Washing Machine
My Shadow and I
Pickle Pickle Pickle Juice
Pirates, Pirates Over the Salt, Salt Sea
Super Sam and the Salad Garden
Tunafish Sandwiches
Where Did That Naughtly Little Hamster Go?

Text Copyright © 1981 by Patty Wolcott Berger
Illustrations Copyright © 1981 by Thomas N. Delaney, III
All Rights Reserved
Addison-Wesley Publishing Company, Inc.
Reading, Massachusetts 01867
Printed in the United States of America

ABCDEFGHIJK-WZ-8987654321

Library of Congress Cataloging in Publication Data

Wolcott, Patty
  EEEEEEK!

  Summary: A lynx captures a fox, a hare, and a
woodpecker to make a stew, but then he falls asleep.
  [1. Animals –Fiction]   I. Delaney, Ned.   II. Title.
PZ7.W8185Ee   [E]   81-3563
ISBN 0-201-08336-1   AACR2

Fox and Hare and
Woodpecker stew.

Fox and Hare and
Woodpecker stew.

Lynx caught Fox.

Eeeeeek!

Hare.

Eeeeeek!

And Lynx caught Hare.

Lynx caught Woodpecker.

Fox and Hare
and Woodpecker stew.
Hare and Fox
and Woodpecker stew.

Lynx slept.
Lynx slept
and slept
and slept.

And Woodpecker pecked.

Woodpecker
pecked and pecked
and pecked.

peck
peck
peck
peck

And Lynx slept.

Woodpecker escaped,
and Hare escaped,
and Fox escaped.

And Lynx slept.

JAMES PRENDERGAST LIBRARY
E
Eeeeeek)

3-1000-0031498 2

E   *Reader*   C.2
Wolcott, Patty.
   Eeeeeek!
                                         5.95

APR 27 1984
JUN 21 1989

JAN 15 2000

SEP 15 2001

JUN 28 2002

JAMES PRENDERGAST
LIBRARY ASSOCIATION

JAMESTOWN, NEW YORK

Member Of

Chautauqua-Cattaraugus Library System